Banff, Moray & Nairn's Lost Rail

by
Gordon Stansfield

The approach to Macduff.

© Gordon Stansfield, 2000
First published in the United Kingdom, 2000,
by Stenlake Publishing, Ochiltree Sawmill, The Lade,
Ochiltree, Ayrshire, KA18 2NX
Telephone / Fax: 01290 423114

ISBN 1 84033 104 6

THE PUBLISHERS REGRET THAT THEY CANNOT SUPPLY
COPIES OF ANY PICTURES FEATURED IN THIS BOOK.

Cornhill Station, 1963.

INTRODUCTION

Today the counties of Banff, Moray and Nairn have just four railway stations between them – Keith, Elgin, Forres and Nairn – and these are linked by just one rail line which runs between Aberdeen and Inverness. This contrasts sharply with the situation one hundred years ago when these counties could boast an additional hundred stations covering nearly two hundred route miles.

The various industries in the three counties – fishing, agriculture, whisky distilling – were all helped to expand by the coming of the railways. The fishing villages on the Moray Firth benefitted enormously and towns such as Lossiemouth were opened up to tourists who flocked in from all over Scotland. The market for malt whisky from the Spey Valley's famous distilleries also expanded. The railway played its part and delivered what it promised. To the ordinary working person the railway opened up new horizons and opportunities. For the first time ever people could travel far and wide at reasonable prices.

Many of the lines in the area were initially built by small companies, but were gradually taken over by the two large rail operators in the North East – the Highland Railway and the Great North of Scotland Railway. These were succeeded in 1923 by the London Midland and Scottish Railway (LMS) and the London and North Eastern Railway (LNER) respectively before finally becoming nationalised in 1948 as British Railways.

Like many other parts of the country, Banff, Moray and Nairn had its fair share of railway oddities such as at Elgin where both the Highland and Great North of Scotland had their own separate stations (although these were linked by a through platform). In the late 1950s with the introduction of railbuses on the Speyside route in order to reduce operating costs and generate more revenue, new halts were opened at long forgotten locations such as Gilbey's Cottages and Imperial Cottages. Nairn Station will be remembered by many even in recent times as the station where the signalman and signalwoman used a push bike to cycle from one end of the station platform to the other in order to change points and signals.

The flexibility of bus services and increasing car ownership led to the railway's demise and although there had been some closures in the 1930s, the cuts of the 1960s finally brought an end to most of the local services. It is hoped, however, that this book will remind people of the days when they played an important part in the everyday life of the region.

Spey Bridge at Garmouth.

Banff – Tillynaught (Tillynaught Junction)

Passenger service withdrawn	6 July 1964	Golf Club House Halt	6 July 1964
Distance	6 miles	Bridgefoot Halt	6 July 1964
Company	Great North of Scotland	Ladysbridge Halt	6 July 1964
		Ordens Halt	6 July 1964
Stations closed	*Date*		
Banff *	6 July 1964	* Known as Banff Harbour until June 1928.

A BR class 2 2-6-0, no. 78045, calls at Bridgefoot Halt with the 8.56 a.m. branch train from Tillynaught to Banff, July 1964.

This line began life in July 1857 when it was authorised as the Banff, Portsoy and Strathisla Railway, but in 1863 the Great North of Scotland took over the running of the line and ownership followed. The branch ran from a junction at Tillynaught Station which was on the Moray Coast Line from Cairnie Junction to Elgin. The branch terminus station remained at Banff even although a short extension over the Deveron Estuary to Macduff could have been undertaken. Services began in August 1859 and for years there were only two stations, Banff and Ladysbridge, which remained the only ones on the line with facilities for freight traffic. In 1913 two halts were opened at Bridgefoot and Golf Club House. The latter was a request halt closed from October to April each year.

LADYSBRIDGE ASYLUM - NEAR BANFF

Boat of Garten (Boat of Garten Junction) – Craigellachie (Craigellachie Junction)

Passenger service withdrawn	18 October 1965
Distance	33.25 miles
Company	Great North of Scotland

Stations closed	*Date*
Nethy Bridge (Inverness-shire) *	18 October 1965
Ballifurth Farm Halt	18 October 1965
Grantown on Spey East **	18 October 1965
Cromdale	18 October 1965
Dalvey Farm Halt	18 October 1965
Dalvey	1 September 1868
Advie (first)	1 September 1868

Stations closed	*Date*
Advie	18 October 1965
Ballindalloch	18 October 1965
Blacksboat	18 October 1965
Knockando ***	18 October 1965
Gilbey's Cottages Halt	18 October 1965
Knockando House Halt ****	18 October 1965
Imperial Cottages Halt	18 October 1965
Carron	18 October 1965
Dailuaine Halt	18 October 1965
Aberlour	18 October 1965

Cromdale Station, ten months after closure, looking towards Grantown.

* Known as Abernethy until 1 November 1867.
** Known as Grantown until 5 June 1950.
*** Known as Dalbealie until 1 May 1905.
**** Previously known as Knockando House
Platform and Knockando.

Work on the line at Knockando, *c.* 1914, with Knockando House Halt in the background

This line, known as the Speyside Line, started its journey north from the Highland Railway at Boat of Garten and ran to Craigellachie where connections could be made for services to Elgin, Keith and Aberdeen. Passenger services began in 1866 and the Highland and Great North of Scotland lines ran parallel with each other until the Highland line turned north-west over Dava Moor for Forres and Inverness. At Grantown on Spey there were two stations – the east belonged to the Great North of Scotland and the west to the Highland. The line passed through some of Scotland's most spectacular scenery and as far back as 1905 the Great North of Scotland ran excursion trains down the line from Aberdeen. The First World War brought new traffic to the line with the establishment of forestry camps at Knockando and Nethy Bridge to provide timber for the country's mines and railways. The London and North Eastern took over the line in 1923 and opened a halt at Dailuaine in 1934 to serve the local distillery. The line also boasted a private station at Knockando House which had a single platform and was not advertised for use by the public. Diesel trains came to the line in 1958 and the then owners, British Railways, opened four halts at Imperial Cottages, Gilbey's Cottages, Dalvey Farm and Ballifurth Farm. However, with the advent of the Beeching Report the line was destined to close. Some remnants remain: Knockando Station is a visitor centre for the Tamdhu Distillery while Aberlour Station is also a visitor centre. The trackbed remains as part of the Speyside Way.

Ballindalloch Station, June 1957. A busy centre for distillery traffic.

Knockando Station, June 1957. A unique feature of this station was an underpass at the north end giving cross-platform access.

The closed station at Carron, August 1966.

Aberlour Station after closure, August 1966. The goods shed is in the centre background.

Elgin (Highland/Great North of Scotland Junction) – Cairnie Junction

Passenger service withdrawn	6 May 1968	*Stations closed*	*Date*
Distance	39 miles	Findochty	6 May 1968
Company	Great North of Scotland	Portknockie	6 May 1968
		Cullen	6 May 1968
Stations closed	*Date*	Tochieneal	1 October 1951
Calcots	6 May 1968	Glassaugh	21 September 1953
Urquhart	6 May 1968	Portsoy (first)	1 April 1884
Garmouth	6 May 1968	Portsoy	6 May 1968
Spey Bay	6 May 1968	Tillynaught	6 May 1968
Portgordon	6 May 1968	Cornhill	6 May 1968
Buckpool	7 March 1960	Glenbarry	6 May 1968
Buckie	6 May 1968	Knock	6 May 1968
Portessie	6 May 1968	Millagan	October 1863

Urquhart Station, 1963. A single platform station typical of the Moray Coast Line.

This line was known as the Moray Firth Coast Line. At Elgin both the Great North of Scotland and the Highland had their own stations and from there passengers could travel west to Inverness, north to Lossiemouth, south to Craigellachie and onwards down the Spey Valley to Boat of Garten and Aviemore or onwards from Craigellachie to Keith. Travelling east towards Aberdeen there was a choice of routes, either the Moray Firth Coast Line or a more direct line to Keith Junction operated by the Highland. The Moray Firth Coast Line served a large number of fishing villages such as Buckie, Cullen and Portgordon and was opened throughout to passengers in 1896. At Portessie a branch of the Highland Railway from Keith used the Great North of Scotland station for the very few trains that traversed this route. Most of the line was single track with passing loops provided at the main stations. Due to the proximity of the line from Orbliston to Fochabers Town, Spey Bay went through several name changes: it was known as Fochabers-on-Spey until November 1883, Fochabers until 1 January 1916, Fochabers and Spey Bay until 1 January 1918, before settling down to the name of Spey Bay. When the London and North Eastern Railway Company took control of the line it introduced a Sunday service, at that time a very rare event in the north of Scotland. When British Railways began operation a through coach was introduced between Glasgow Buchanan Street and Elgin along the line on summer Saturdays and this service survived until 1962. Cairnie Junction Station was where the line joined the present day route for trains between Inverness and Aberdeen. Like one or two other stations in Scotland this was an exchange platform only and had no provision for passengers other than those arriving by rail. Some of the Moray Firth route survives as a walkway with a few of the line's viaducts still remaining, for example at Cullen and over the Spey at Garmouth.

A BR Type 2 diesel engine, no. 6150, with the 1.52 p.m. service from Elgin to Aberdeen at Spey Bay Station, August 1966.

A BR standard 2-6-4T, no. 80021, at Portgordon with the 3.45 p.m. train from Aberdeen to Elgin, August 1959.

Buckpool Station, 1958. A single platform station serving a suburb of Buckie.

Buckie Station, 1958.

Portknockie Station, 1958. This was a typical pine-built GNSR station with passing loop.

The curved platform of Cullen Station, 1963. The house on the right, beyond the station building, was a typical L-plan stationmaster's home.

Portsoy Station, *c.* **1910. The original station of the Banff, Portsoy and Strathisla Railway is on the far right, behind the telegraph pole (it later became a goods shed). There was a branch line to the harbour on the east side of this building but it ceased to be used in the 1880s.**

Tillynaught Station, August 1956, looking towards Portsoy. The coastal line is on the left while on the right is a service to Banff.

Elgin (South Junction) – Keith Junction

Passenger service withdrawn	6 May 1968
Distance	27.5 miles
Company	Great North of Scotland

Stations closed	Date
Longmorn	6 May 1968
Coleburn *	After July 1926
Birchfield Halt	7 May 1956
Rothes	6 May 1968

Stations closed	Date
Dandaleith	5 March 1962
Craigellachie **	6 May 1968
Dufftown	6 May 1968
Drummuir Curling Pond Platform	Date unknown
Drummuir	6 May 1968
Towiemore Halt	6 May 1968
Auchindachy ***	6 May 1968
Keith Town ****	6 May 1968

Longmorn Station, August 1966.

* Known as Coleburn's Platform until April 1867.
** Known as Strathspey Junction until June 1864 and then Craigellachie Junction until about 1904.

*** Known as Botriphne until October 1862.
**** Known as Earlsmill until May 1897.

Rothes Station served a number of local distilleries.

The line from Elgin to Keith Junction via Craigellachie was an alternative route to two others for travel between Inverness and Aberdeen. These were the Moray Firth coast route which closed to passengers on the same date and the more direct Highland Railway route which is still in use today. The line from Elgin joined the Boat of Garten Speyside line at Craigellachie and between there and Keith Junction, the line followed in part the gorge of the Fiddich which involved the construction of two bridges. The fact that two routes ran via Elgin and Keith Junction resulted in difficult operational problems in the latter part of the nineteenth century and attempts were made to rationalise and improve services between the Highland and the Great North of Scotland. However, an attempt to amalgamate the two companies amalgamation services for the line came to nothing. After the closure of the line as far as Craigellachie, the track to Dufftown from Keith Junction remained and during the summer carried the 'Northern Belle', a special train which ran from Aberdeen to Dufftown allowing the passengers to visit a distillery in the area and also enjoy dinner on the train whilst it remained stationary. This service continued until March 1991 when, because of the financial cost of chartering from British Rail, it was withdrawn.

A service to Aviemore at Craigellachie's Speyside Platform.

A former GNSR (later LNER) 4-4-0 at the Speyside platform of Craigellachie Station with a service to Boat of Garten.

Drummuir Station, 1957.

Towiemore Station, August 1966. It was still open at the time – the carriage body served as a waiting room!

The sheds at Keith.

Findhorn – Kinloss

Passenger service withdrawn	1 January 1869
Distance	3 miles
Company	Inverness and Aberdeen Junction

Station closed	*Date*
Findhorn	1 January 1869

Known as the Findhorn Railway, this branch line was first opened for traffic on 18 April 1860, just one day short of a year after its creation by an Act of Parliament. Passenger services were withdrawn on 1 January 1869 although freight services continued until 1890. At Findhorn the passenger station was situated on the quayside but the subsequent silting up of the harbour led to the closure of the line due to a reduction in traffic. Train services continued to serve Kinloss until 3 May 1965, although services still pass through the closed station *en route* from Inverness to Aberdeen.

Fochabers Town – Orbliston Junction

Passenger service withdrawn	14 September 1931	*Stations closed*	*Date*
Distance	3 miles	Fochabers Town	14 September 1931
Company	Highland	Balnacoul Halt	14 September 1931

The closed station of Fochabers Town, 1958. This was a terminal station, close to Baxter's factory, on the opposite side of the Spey from the town.

Situated on the line from Inverness to Aberdeen this branch was opened by the Highland on 16 October 1893. The Highland's line from Elgin to Keith (still in use) had a station called Fochabers although the actual town was about three miles away and when this branch was opened, Fochabers had its name changed to Orbliston Junction. There was further difficulty as the Great North of Scotland also had a station known as Fochabers on its line from Elgin to Cairnie Junction via the Moray Firth coast towns. Due to this the Highland decided to name the branch line terminus Fochabers Town although the town was almost half a mile away. The Great North of Scotland changed the name of its Fochabers station to Spey Bay in 1919. The branch remained open to freight traffic until March 1966.

Forres: East Junction – South Junction

Passenger service withdrawn	18 October 1965
Distance	0.25 miles
Company	Highland

The station at Forres was triangular shaped in order to be able to accommodate trains running between Inverness and Aberdeen as well as trains going south to Aviemore via Dava. Some of these trains may have originated from stations to the east of Forres. The section of line between the east and south junctions allowed trains coming from the Elgin direction to travel on to the Forres to Aviemore line. Although this short spur closed in tandem with the Forres to Aviemore line, it remained open for goods traffic until May 1967.

Forres (West Junction) – Aviemore (Aviemore Junction)

Passenger service withdrawn	18 October 1965
Distance	35.75 miles
Company	Highland

Stations closed	*Date*
Rafford	31 May 1865
Dunphail	18 October 1965

Stations closed	*Date*
Dava	18 October 1965
Castle Grant Platform	Date unknown
Grantown on Spey West *	18 October 1965
Broomhill (Inverness-shire)	18 October 1965
Boat of Garten (Inverness-shire) **	18 October 1965

Dunphail Station.

* Known as Grantown until 1 June 1912 and then Grantown on Spey until 5 June 1950.
** Reopened on 22 July 1978 by the Strathspey Railway Preservation Society who operate a service to Aviemore.

Opened on 3 August 1863 this line provided the first through service between Perth and Inverness, joining the Inverness to Aberdeen line at Forres. This status remained until 1898 when the shorter route to Inverness from Aviemore via Carr Bridge was opened. The line over Dava summit was steeply graded and was prone to severe snow drifts in the winter months. There were three trains in each direction in 1922 with the journey time being about an hour and a quarter. Castle Grant Platform was for private use by the Grant family on whose land the railway ran, and was not available to the general public.

Grantown on Spey West Station in the 1950s.

Grange (Station Junction) – Grange North Junction

Passenger service withdrawn	7 March 1960
Distance	0.75 miles
Company	Great North of Scotland

This line was known as the Grange Curve and linked the Moray Firth Coast Line at Grange North Junction with Grange Station on the section of line from Cairnie Junction to Keith Junction which today forms part of the route taken by Aberdeen to Inverness trains. When the Moray Firth Coast Line opened to passengers in July 1859 trains had to call at Grange Station as there was no link between the coast line and Cairnie Junction. This involved trains reversing at Grange Station and the situation was not remedied until 1886 when a half mile link was brought into use although authorisation had not been approved. This meant that the original line carried fewer passenger trains. The only ones which used the loop were those to and from the coast line going south along the Strathspey route from Keith Junction to Craigellachie and Aviemore. These were withdrawn in March 1960.

Hopeman – Alves (Alves Junction)

Passenger service withdrawn	14 September 1931
Distance	7.5 miles
Company	Highland

Stations closed	Date
Hopeman *	14 September 1931
Cummingston	1 April 1904
Burghead (first)	10 October 1892
Burghead	14 September 1931
Coltfield Platform	14 September 1931

* Closed from 1 January 1917 until 1918 or 1919.

A special railtour service at the closed station of Burghead, 1960.

Burghead in its heyday.

Railway Station. Burghead.

J. Cummins, Burghead.

This branch line in the north east of Scotland was opened in two stages. The first from Alves on the present day route from Inverness to Aberdeen opened on 22 December 1862 when it ran to a passenger station located on Burghead Pier. The second section was opened from Burghead to Hopeman on 10 October 1892. Due to this a new station was built at Burghead. The passenger service was about average for a highland branch line. In 1922 there were six weekday arrival and departures between Alves and Hopeman, including one short working to Burghead. Freight services between Burghead and Hopeman were withdrawn in 1957 while those between Alves and Burghead lasted until November 1966.

Lossiemouth – Elgin (Lossie Junction)

Passenger service withdrawn	6 April 1964		*Stations closed*	*Date*
Distance	4.5 miles		Lossiemouth	6 April 1964
Company	Great North of Scotland		Greens of Drainie	November 1859
			Linksfield Level Crossing	November 1859

Lossiemouth Station with the Station Hotel and booking office on the right-hand side.

The Lossiemouth branch line was opened to passengers in August 1852 and it began at Lossie Junction on the Moray Firth Coast Line, heading directly northwards to Lossiemouth. Apart from connections being available at Elgin for trains to Aberdeen and Inverness there were through coaches to certain locations on some of the trains to and from Lossiemouth. In 1923 a sleeping car service was provided between Lossiemouth and London Kings Cross via Aberdeen and the east coast main line. It had a very early departure time – 4.30 *in the afternoon*. The total mileage of the service was 630 miles, making it the longest through journey of any train until 1984 when British Rail introduced a service from Edinburgh to Penzance (the sleeping car service was withdrawn at the outbreak of the Second World War). The two intermediate stations on the line only lasted seven years after the line opened; they were only opened in an attempt to attract passengers from the nearby farms and were never provided with any proper station buildings. Freight services lasted until March 1966.

Macduff – Inveramsay (Inveramsay Junction) *

		Stations closed	Date
Passenger service withdrawn	1 October 1951	Macduff	1 October 1951
Distance	29.75 miles	Banff Bridge	1 October 1951
Company	Great North of Scotland	Banff & Macduff	1 July 1872

Banff Bridge Station, 1960. This station gave direct access to Aberdeen whereas the harbour station gave an indirect connection south.

This branch line left the present day Inverness to Aberdeen route at Inveramsay Junction where a station was built to accommodate the new traffic on the line. Opened as far as Turriff in 1857, the line was not extended to Macduff until three years later. Unfortunately the station at Macduff was three quarters of a mile from the town and it took twelve years before a better located station, known as Macduff, was built. Banff Bridge was opened at the same time to serve the people of Banff. The line was closed completely from Macduff to Turriff in 1961 and from Turriff to Inveramsay in January 1966.

* Closed stations on this line that were in Aberdeenshire were King Edward, Plaidy, Turriff, Auchterless, Fyvie, Rothie-Norman and Wartle.

Macduff was a terminal station with splendid coastal views.

MACDUFF, from Hill of Doune.

Portessie – Keith (Keith Junction West)

Passenger service withdrawn	9 August 1915	*Stations closed*	*Date*
Distance	13.5 miles	Rathven	9 August 1915
Company	Highland	Drybridge Platform	9 August 1915
		Enzie	9 August 1915
Stations closed	*Date*	Aultmore *	9 August 1915
Portessie	9 August 1915		
Buckie	9 August 1915	* Known as Forgie until January 1899.	

A preserved Highland Railway 4-6-0, no. 103, approaching Aultmore with a special railtour service from Keith Junction, June 1962.

Opened in August 1884, this line was designed mainly to capture a share of the rich fishing traffic as well as the farming trade in the area. The line joined the Great North of Scotland Moray Firth line at Portessie and there the Highland used the same station complex as the Great North of Scotland. Although the passenger service was withdrawn in 1915 it had been intended to reinstate the service after the end of the First World War and the station buildings remained intact and were not demolished. An oddity which arose after the line had been closed was that a ten mile section of track between Buckie and Aultmore had been removed thus leaving a section of the track at either end which was used for freight traffic. In 1924, under London Midland and Scottish control, the track was relaid with a view to reopening the line but this never took place as the traffic levels were reassessed and found to be low. The section between Keith to Aultmore remained open to freight until October 1966 and between Buckie to Portessie until April 1944.

Rothes – Orton

Passenger service withdrawn	1 August 1866
Distance	3.25 miles
Company	Great North of Scotland

Station closed	*Date*
Sourden	1 August 1866

This line opened to passengers in August 1858. At that time Rothes was not linked by rail to Elgin and due to this a branch was built to link Rothes with Orton which was on the Highland Railway line from Elgin to Keith. However, when the section of line from Rothes to Elgin was opened in 1862 the Great North of Scotland decided to withdraw the service. This caused considerable unrest as no notice of withdrawal was given. At Orton the junction with the Highland line was removed and only a freight service was provided between Rothes and Sourden siding. For many years the line lay forgotten and it was not until 1907 that the track was lifted.

Closed passenger stations on lines still open to passenger services

Line/Service	Inverness – Aberdeen *	Station	*Date of closure*
		Alves	3 May 1965
Station	· *Date of closure*	Mosstowie	7 March 1955
Kildrummie Platform **	1899	Lhanbryde	7 December 1964
Auldearn	6 June 1960	Orbliston ***	7 December 1964
Brodie	3 May 1965	Orton	7 December 1964
Kinloss (first)	18 April 1860	Mulben	7 December 1964
Kinloss (second)	May 1904	Taucher's Platform	7 December 1964
Kinloss (third)	3 May 1965	Grange	6 May 1968

* Closed stations on this line which were in Inverness-shire were Allanfearn, Castle Stuart Platform, Dalcross and Gollanfield. In Banffshire the stations closed were Rothiemay and Cairnie Junction, while in Aberdeenshire they were Gartly, Kennethmont, Wardhouse, Buchanstone, Oyne, Pitcaple, Inveramsay, Inverurie (first), Kintore, Kinaldie, Pitmedden, Dyce (first), Dyce, Stoneywood, Bankhead, Bucksburn, Persley Halt, Woodside, Don Street, Kittybrewster, Hutchieson Street and Schoolhill.

** Known as Cawdor until 1 January 1857 and Kildrummie until 1858.

*** Known as Fochabers until 16 October 1893 and then Orbliston Junction until 12 September 1960.

Auldearn Station, c. 1930. A badly sited station some distance from the village.

The closed station at Kinloss (third and last), 1975. In the background trees mark the site of the original Kinloss Station and the branch to Findhorn, an early closure.

Alves Station, 1933.

Orbliston Station. Many will remember the call 'Change for Fochabers Town' at the platform to the left of the station building.

Mulben Station.